Jack, Leslie & Lily

from

THIS BOOK IS PRESENTED TO:

_____

ON:

_____

BY:

_____

K-LOVE BOOKS

K-LOVE Books
5700 West Oaks Blvd
Rocklin, CA 95765

Buy 1 Copy, Give 1 Copy Free

Each time a copy of *Bible Stories & Prayers* is purchased a ministry
edition will be given away free of charge through one of our partner
ministries. For more information, visit our website at TheBibleforMe.com.

Printed in China

First edition: 2022
10 9 8 7 6 5 4 3 2 1

Names: Parker, Amy, 1976-, author. | Nawrocki, Mike, author. | Thompson, Taylor, illustrator.
Title: Bible for me : stories and prayers / written by Amy Parker and Mike Nawrocki;
illustrated by Taylor Thompson.
Description: Franklin, TN: K-LOVE Books/Brentwood Studios, 2021. | Summary: Throughout
these fifty favorite Bible stories, children will come face-to-face with God's endless love for them,
providing a firm foundation of faith to last a lifetime.
Identifiers: ISBN: 978-1-954201-21-7 (hardcover) | 978-1-954201-22-4 (ebook) |
978-1-954201-23-1 (audio)
Subjects: LCSH Bible stories. | BISAC JUVENILE NONFICTION / Religion / Bible Stories / General
Classification: LCC BS551.2 .P372 2021 | DDC 220.9/505--dc23

Project management by Dan Lynch, Brentwood Studios
Interior design by Diana Lawrence
Edited by Julie Monroe
Theological review by Doug Powell and Zac Settle

Visit or contact us at TheBibleforMe.com

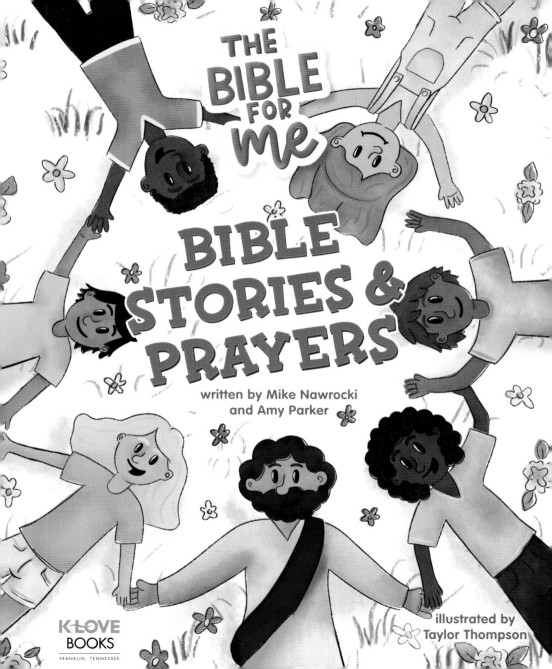

THE BIBLE FOR ME

BIBLE STORIES & PRAYERS

written by Mike Nawrocki
and Amy Parker

illustrated by
Taylor Thompson

K-LOVE
BOOKS
FRANKLIN, TENNESSEE

Dear Reader,

Thank you for choosing to share these Bible stories. We know that an early understanding of God's Word plays a vital role in establishing a lifelong foundation of faith, and we thank you for making that a priority for the children in your life.

Bible Stories & Prayers, as part of the Bible for Me series, was written to speak directly to the listeners, your children, and to tell God's story in a way that reveals His love for each of them.

We hope not only to convey the original power and timelessness of each story, but also to emphasize how personal and relevant the story is to each child's life. Every story ends with a prayer that enables you (the reader) to substitute your child's name for the words marked in blue, making the story uniquely personal.

We hope that after reading *Bible Stories & Prayers* children will understand God's endless love for them, providing a firm foundation of faith to last a lifetime.

Mike & Amy

Here's an example of how you can make the prayers at the end of each story personal for your child.

Dear God,

Thank You for sending Jesus to take away our sins. Please help us always remember Him and what He has done for us. Amen.

Dear God,

Thank You for sending Jesus to take away our sins. Please help Amy always remember Him and what He has done for her. Amen.

Old Testament Bible Stories

New Testament Bible Stories

Dear Child,

Do you know that God loves you and has a plan for you? He does! Do you know that He had His story written down for you? He did!

He loves you so much that over the entire history of God's people, He inspired His followers to write their story, His story. When we read this big story, we learn so much about who God is, about how our character should look like His, and how deep and wide and endless His love is for us.

In this book you will read fifty stories from the Bible, retold in a way that will help you understand the amazing characteristics of God and His story. These stories will show you God's glorious power, His faithfulness, and how He has loved and guided His people over the centuries. As you read and learn more about God, you will see how the Bible is your story too. You will learn how you fit in and how these stories, and the whole Bible, apply to your life today.

As you read or listen to these stories, please remember that these are stories for you, given to you by a God who loves you so very much.

In His love,

Mike & Amy

OLD
TESTAMENT

The Very Beginning

(Genesis 1-2)

Did you know that there was never a time when God didn't exist? Isn't that amazing?

In the very beginning, God made all the heavens and all the earth.

At first, the earth was empty and dark. But God said, "Let there be light." And light burst out of the dark and empty. God saw that the light was good, and He called it "day." He called the darkness "night." That was the first day of Creation.

On the second day, God made the skies. On the third day, He separated the water into oceans and made dry land.

Then He made every kind of plant and tree, fruit and vegetable. God saw that this was good.

On day four, God made the sun
and the moon and the stars. They
would give light, day and night,
and show the seasons too.

On the fifth day, God made fish to splash in the ocean and birds to fly through the skies. God thought that this was all good.

On day six, God made mooing cows and chirping crickets—animals and insects in every shape and size.

But He wasn't finished yet!

15

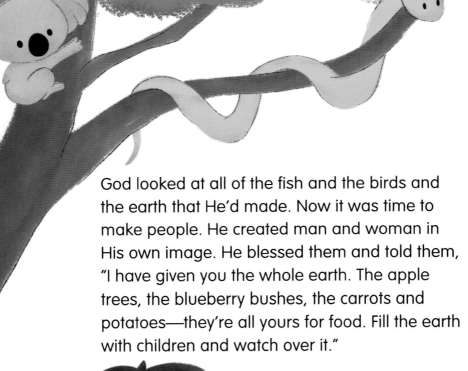

God looked at all of the fish and the birds and the earth that He'd made. Now it was time to make people. He created man and woman in His own image. He blessed them and told them, "I have given you the whole earth. The apple trees, the blueberry bushes, the carrots and potatoes—they're all yours for food. Fill the earth with children and watch over it."

God saw that all He had created was so, so good.

Finally, God's work of Creation was finished. The sun, the moon, and the heavenly stars hung in the sky. Whales and minnows splashed in the oceans and rivers. Animals roamed the mountains and valleys. Vegetables and fruits and vines and flowers covered the earth. And there were humans, made in God's own image, to look after it all.

On the seventh day, God rested. He blessed that day and made it holy.

Dear God,

Thank You for making us! Thank You for making all the animals on land and in the sea. Thank You for making yummy fruits and vegetables for us to eat. Help us take good care of the earth and ourselves. Amen.

17

Adam and Eve Mess Up

(Genesis 2-3)

God loves us even when we choose to do wrong.
He always has, even from the beginning.

God shaped the first man from nothing but
dust. When God breathed life into that dust,
man came to life.

God gave this man a beautiful garden to live in called Eden. God told him to take care of the garden and to eat from any tree except one.

"Do not eat from the tree of the knowledge of good and evil," God said. "If you do, you will die."

Then God said, "It isn't good for this man to be alone. He needs someone to help him." So God put him into a deep sleep, took one of his ribs, and created another person. The man said, "I will call her 'woman' because she was made from my body."

One day a sneaky serpent spoke to Eve. He said, "Did God really tell you that you can't eat from any tree in the garden?"

"We can eat fruit from any tree," Eve said, "just not the tree in the middle of the garden. We can't even touch it or we will die."

"You won't die!" the snake said. "If you eat that juicy, delicious fruit, you will know good from evil, just like God."

Eve looked over at the tree again. She wondered if the fruit would really make her as smart as God. She took the fruit and ate it. She gave it to Adam, and he ate some too.

That evening Adam and Eve heard God walking through the garden, and they hid.

"Where are you?" God called.

Adam answered, "I heard You coming, so I hid behind this tree."

God asked, "Did you eat from the tree that I told you not to eat from?"

"Yes, Eve gave it to me!" Adam answered.

"The snake tricked me!" Eve said.

So God punished the snake. And He punished Adam and Eve.

God continued to care for them, of course. But because they broke God's rule, Adam and Eve were no longer allowed to live in the garden that God had given them.

Dear God,

Thank You for loving us, even when we choose to do wrong. Please help us follow Your rules. And thank You for sending us Jesus to forgive our sins. Amen.

God Starts Over

(Genesis 6-9)

Do you know that you can *always* trust God?
Thankfully for all people and animals alive today,
Noah trusted God and followed His directions.

Many years after Adam and Eve, people had forgotten about God and were doing lots of terrible things. Everyone, that is, except for Noah.

God told Noah that He wanted to start over and would send a great flood to cover the earth.

But God promised that He would keep Noah and his family safe. He told Noah to build a boat big enough for his family and every kind of animal.

Noah trusted God and got to work.

It took Noah many, many years to build the giant ark. Noah may have wondered if a flood would ever come, but he kept on building.

When he finished, he filled the great ship with food and supplies. God then told Noah, his family, and the animals to get into the ark. When everyone was on board, God closed the door.

Before long, underground waters
sprung from the earth, and rain
poured from the sky! The whole earth,
to the top of the tallest mountain, was
swallowed up in water.

But Noah and his family were
safe inside the ark. They cared
for all the animals as the ark
floated on the waves.

Noah trusted God and waited.

After many months, Noah opened a
window he had made in the ark and
released a dove. The dove returned with
a freshly plucked leaf from an olive tree
in its beak. The earth was finally dry.

Then God said to Noah, "Come out of the ark with your family and all the animals so that they can be fruitful and multiply throughout the earth."

God had kept His promise.

God then placed a rainbow in the sky and made one more promise. "Never again will a flood destroy the earth."

Dear God,

Thank You for loving us and for taking care of us the way You took care of Noah. Help us trust You every day the way Noah trusted You. Also, thank You for animals. They are super cool. Amen.

God's Promise to Abraham

(Genesis 12-13, 15, 17-18, 21)

**God always keeps His promises—
even when they seem impossible!**

Noah's family filled the earth, just as God had said. Many years later, God spoke to a man named Abram. He asked him to leave his home and travel to another land. God didn't tell Abram where he was going. God just promised to show him the way.

After a long journey, Abram pitched his tent by some tall oak trees. There, God called to him.

"Abram, come. Look at the stars."

"I see them, Lord."

"Try to count them."

Abram stared at the thousands and thousands of twinkles in the deep blue sky.

"That is how big your family will be. Your children and their children and their children will grow to be as many as the stars in the sky."

When Abram was ninety-nine years old, God appeared to him again.

"From now on, your name will be Abraham," God said. "Your wife, Sarai, will be called Sarah. She will have a son named Isaac, and she will be the mother of nations and kings."

But how can this happen? We are so old, Abraham wondered.

Soon after, three men came to Abraham's home. "This time next year Sarah will have a son," one of the men said.

Listening from the tent, Sarah laughed. "How could I have a son at this age?"

The Lord asked Abraham, "Why did Sarah laugh? Is there anything I can't do?"

A year later, when Abraham was one hundred years old, Sarah and Abraham's first son was born. They named him Isaac, which means "laughter."

Even though Sarah had laughed at the idea of having a child at her age, she now held that baby in her arms.

God will always keep His promises— even when they seem impossible!

Dear God,

Thank You for keeping Your promises. Help us always know that Your promises are true. Amen.

Abraham Gives His Best

(Genesis 22)

Did you know that God wants
our very best? He does!

When Isaac was a boy, God told Abraham, "Take your son, Isaac, and go to the mountains. I will show you where to go. When you get there, offer your son as a sacrifice to Me."

Early the next morning, Abraham did exactly what God had asked him to do. He saddled his donkey. He split wood for the fire. He gathered two helpers and his son. And together, they all set out for the mountains.

After traveling for three days, Abraham told his helpers, "Isaac and I are going to that mountain to worship. Stay here with the donkey, and we'll come back when we're finished."

Abraham unloaded the wood and gave it to Isaac to carry. Then Abraham took the knife and the fire and led the way.

After they had walked for a while, Isaac said, "Father, we have the fire and the wood, but where is the lamb that we're going to sacrifice?"

Abraham answered, "God will provide the lamb, my son."

Soon they arrived at the place God had shown Abraham. Abraham built an altar for the sacrifice, arranged the wood, and then he looked at his son. Isaac was the promise from God that Abraham had waited many years to receive. But Abraham was willing to give God his most cherished gift.

"Abraham, wait!" a voice called from heaven. "You don't need to do this. Now I know that you wouldn't keep even your son from Me."

Abraham looked up and saw something rustling in the bushes. It was a ram.

God provided the sacrifice that day because He had seen that Abraham was willing to give God his absolute best.

Dear God,

Please help us always give You our best. Help us to put You first and to be willing to give up even our favorite things to follow You. Amen.

Jacob's and Esau's Blessings

(Genesis 24–25, 27)

God knows our future. He knew
the future of Jacob and Esau, and
He knows your future too!

When Abraham was very old, he sent a helper to find a wife for Isaac. God showed the man Rebekah.

After Isaac and Rebekah were married, God blessed them with twins. Rebekah could feel the babies wrestling in her belly and asked God why they were fighting.

"From your boys will come two different nations," God told her. "The older son will serve the younger son."

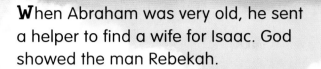

When the babies were born, the first son, Esau, had red hair all over his body. The second son was named Jacob.

As they grew up, Jacob was quiet and stayed home, and Esau spent time in the fields hunting.

One day Esau came in from hunting and saw Jacob cooking stew. Esau was so tired and so hungry. He asked Jacob for some of his food.

"Okay," Jacob said, "but first promise me your birthright." Because Esau was the oldest brother, he would get more rights and property than Jacob when their father died.

"Fine," Esau said. "I'm going to die if I don't eat, and the birthright will be no use to me then!"

Isaac grew older and older until he could no longer see. He said to Esau, "Son, I don't know how much longer I'll be with you. Go hunting and prepare a delicious meal for me. Then I will bless you before I die."

When Esau left, Rebekah told Jacob, "We will make a meal for him that he loves, and then he will give you the blessing instead." Jacob put on Esau's clothes and put fur on his arms so that he would smell and feel like Esau.

"Father, it's me, Esau," Jacob said. "I've cooked you a meal so that you can bless me."

Isaac felt his son's skin and smelled his clothes. "Esau," he said, "may the Lord bless you with plenty. May your brother and people and nations bow down to you. Blessed are those who bless you."

Soon Esau returned from hunting. He asked his father to bless him.

"But I have already blessed the son who brought the meal to me."

Esau realized what had happened and became very upset. "Father, bless me too!"

Isaac did bless Esau, but the older son would serve the younger. And the words God had spoken to Rebekah would come true.

Dear God,

Thank You for knowing what our future will be. Thank You for having good plans for us. Please help us see and follow those plans. Amen.

Joseph Helps His Brothers

(Genesis 37, 39-45)

Did you know that God can make everything work out for good? He did it for Joseph, and He can do it for you!

Jacob had twelve sons, and Joseph was his favorite.

Joseph's ten older brothers didn't like him very much. They were not happy when their father gave Joseph a colorful robe as a special gift.

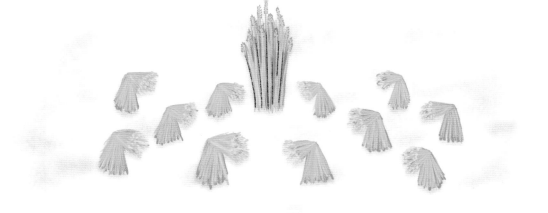

Joseph also dreamed that his brothers would bow down to him one day. When he told his brothers about his dream, they liked Joseph even less.

So they took Joseph's robe and threw him into a pit. Then they sold Joseph to some traders.

When they showed their father Joseph's tattered robe, Jacob cried. "Oh no! Something awful must have happened to him!"

The traders sold Joseph to an officer named Potiphar in Egypt. But there, Joseph was put in jail for something he didn't do.

Even in jail, God was with Joseph. Joseph explained dreams for the king's servants.

Then, when the king had a dream about fat cows and skinny cows, he asked Joseph to explain it.

"I can't tell you," Joseph told him, "but God can."

Joseph said, "There is going to be a season with lots of food, but then there will be a season with no food."

The king told Joseph, "Since God has told you about this famine, you are the best person to prepare for it." He put Joseph in charge of all of Egypt. He was second only to the king.

For years, Joseph stocked up grain. And when the famine came, Egypt was prepared.

In Canaan, Jacob and his sons were running out of food. He sent his ten older sons to buy grain in Egypt. Benjamin, the youngest, stayed home. When they met with the ruler to buy food, they bowed before him. They did not recognize Joseph.

"Spies!" Joseph yelled, not revealing who he was. "If you're really who you say you are, go back and get your younger brother you told me about!"

So the brothers went home and got Benjamin. When they returned, Joseph told his brothers who he was. The brothers were afraid. They thought Joseph would want to punish them for selling him to the traders.

However, Joseph told his brothers, "You tried to hurt me, but God used that for our good. Go home, get our father, and bring him here. Together, we will have all the food and land we will ever need."

Dear God,

Thank You for taking care of us. Thank You for helping even the bad things work out for good. Amen.

Baby Moses Is Saved

(Exodus 1–2)

God is always watching over us. He watched over Moses, and He will watch over you!

A lot of time passed, and a lot changed after Jacob's family moved to Egypt. Although Jacob and his sons had died many years ago, their children had children, and his family, the Israelites, grew and grew. But now they were all slaves.

So much time had passed that the new pharaoh, the king of Egypt, didn't really know Jacob or Joseph or their family. But there were so many Israelites that he was afraid they would win if there was ever a war. So he made a rule to get rid of all the baby boys born to Israelite families.

One Israelite family tried very hard to keep their baby boy hidden. But after three months, they realized that they just couldn't hide him anymore.

The mother carefully chose a little basket and covered it with tar and pitch to protect it from the water. She placed her baby in the basket and set it in the tall grass by the bank of the Nile River. The boy's sister, Miriam, watched nearby.

When Pharaoh's daughter went to the Nile to bathe, she noticed the basket in the grass. She asked a helper to bring it to her. When she opened it, she saw a baby boy crying.

"This must be one of the Israelite babies," she said.

Miriam quickly stepped up. "Would you like for me to find a woman to take care of him for you?"

"Please do," she answered.

Miriam ran to get her mother. Then they hurried back together.

"I'll pay you to take care of him until he's older," the princess said.

So the baby's mother gladly cared for her son until she had to return him to the palace.

When she did, Pharaoh's daughter said, "I'll name him Moses because I pulled him from the water."

So Moses, an Israelite boy, grew up in the safety of Pharaoh's palace.

Dear God,

Thank You for watching over our family. Thank You for keeping us safe. Amen.

God Calls Moses

(Exodus 2-4)

God always helps us do His work, just like
He helped Moses do a big, important job!

After Moses grew up, he got into some trouble
with Pharaoh in Egypt and ran away to Midian.
He stayed there and married a woman named
Zipporah. He helped her father take care of his
sheep.

One day while Moses was out with the sheep, they walked by a mountain. That's when Moses saw the strangest sight. It was a bush, blazing with fire, but it was not burning up. Moses went to get a closer look.

"Moses!" a voice called from the bush.

"I'm here!" Moses answered.

"Take off your sandals. You are on holy ground! I am the God of Abraham, Isaac, and Jacob. I have heard My people's cries from Egypt. And I'm going to send you to save them."

"Me?" Moses looked up.

"I will be with you," God told him.

"But what will I tell them?"

"Tell them I sent you."

"But they won't believe me."

God told Moses to throw his staff on the ground. Moses threw down his long stick, and it turned into a snake!

"Now pick it up," God said.

Moses picked it up by the tail, and it turned back into a staff.

"When they see this, they will know I have sent you."

"But, Lord," Moses said, "I'm not a good speaker."

"Who made the mouth? I did. And I will be with you," God said.

"But, Lord, please ask someone else to go."

"Okay, Moses. Your brother, Aaron, is a good speaker," God told him. "He will go with you. And I will be with you both."

So Moses went to meet his Aaron.

God would be with them all the way and help them do what He had called them to do.

Dear God,

Thank You for allowing us to help with Your plans. Help us remember that You are always with us, helping us do what You created us to do. Amen.

God Splits the Red Sea

(Exodus 4–15)

Did you know that the Lord will fight for you? He fought for His people, and He is fighting for them still!

Moses and Aaron went to Egypt, taking the staff as proof of God's miracles. They told Pharaoh, "The Lord God of Israel said, 'Let My people go.'"

"Who is the Lord?" Pharaoh asked. "Why should I listen to Him?" The Israelites were Pharaoh's slaves, and he didn't want to let them go.

"He is the God of the Israelites," Moses and Aaron said. "Let us go and worship Him."

"No! Who will do all of their work?" Pharaoh asked.

God said to Moses, "Tell him I will turn the water to blood. Then he will know that I am the Lord."

But even after the water turned to blood, Pharaoh did not listen.

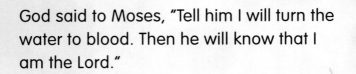

God sent frogs and gnats and flies and sickness and sores. He sent hail and locusts and darkness. But Pharaoh still wouldn't let God's people go.

"I will send one last plague," God explained. "Tell the Israelites to prepare a perfect lamb for dinner. If they brush the lamb's blood around their door, I will pass over that house. The plague will not harm them."

That night, cries rang out from every Egyptian home. Their firstborn sons and firstborn livestock had died.

"Go!" Pharaoh told Moses. "Take your people and go!"

The Israelites quickly left Egypt and set up camp by the Red Sea.

Then Pharaoh changed his mind. "Get the horses and the chariots!" he ordered. "Let's go get our slaves back!"

The Israelites woke to an army thundering toward them. "What have you done?" they said to Moses. "You brought us out here to die!"

"Don't be afraid," Moses said. "The Lord will fight for you!"

God told Moses to stretch out his staff over the sea. When he did, a strong wind divided the sea, creating a dry path in the middle, between two walls of water. The Israelites were amazed and walked safely through the sea to the other side.

In the morning, they saw the Egyptian army still racing after them, down the path through the sea.

"Stretch your hand over the sea," God said. When Moses did, the waters of the sea came crashing down on the Egyptian army.

The Israelites saw that they were safe, and they began to sing. They praised God for saving them, His chosen people. And soon He would lead them into a new land, a home of their own.

Dear God,

Thank You for fighting for us. And thank You for sending Jesus, the perfect Lamb, to save us from our sins. Amen.

Moses on the Mountain

(Exodus 19-20)

Your parents give you rules because
they love you and want the very best for you.
Because of His great love for us, God also
gives His children rules.

After Moses and the Israelites crossed through
the Red Sea, they walked for weeks through a
huge, hot desert to the foot of Mount Sinai, one
of the tallest mountains in all of Egypt.

Moses climbed up the mountain to talk with God. There, God reminded Moses of all He had done for the Israelites and how much He loved them. God said that if the Israelites would love and obey Him and follow His commandments, they would be His own special family.

Moses told the Israelites what God had said. "Sure!" they said. "His own special family? That sounds amazing! We will do what God tells us to do!"

Moses went back up the mountain again. This time smoke billowed down from the hills. Thunder roared and lightning flashed, and the whole mountain shook as the Israelites gathered at the bottom.

God gave Moses and the people ten instructions for loving Him and for loving one another.

The commandments were written on stone tablets. Moses carried the stones down the mountain and showed them to the people of Israel.

1. You must have no other god but Me.

2. Do not make idols to worship.

3. Do not misuse My name.

4. Dedicate one day a week to resting and worshiping Me.

5. Honor your father and mother.

6. Do not kill each other.

7. Be faithful to your wife or husband.

8. Do not steal from each other.

9. Do not lie to each other.

10. Do not be jealous of each other.

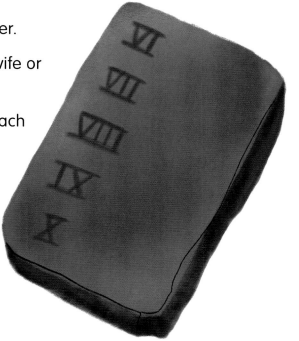

Dear God,

Thank You for loving us and telling us how to love You and to love others. Even though we cannot always follow Your instructions perfectly, thank You for sending Your perfect Son, Jesus, so that we can be part of Your family forever. Amen.

Exploring Canaan

(Numbers 13-14)

God wants the very best for His people. He wanted the best for the Israelites, and He wants it for me and you!

After the Israelites had been traveling for some time, they arrived near the land of Canaan. God told Moses, "Send twelve men, one from each tribe of Israel, to explore Canaan, the land I am giving to My people."

As the men explored, they found a grape cluster so huge that two men had to carry it! They also saw pomegranates and figs. They took the fruit with them for the Israelites to see.

After forty days, they returned and showed the people the fruit. They told them how rich and plentiful the land was.

"But," some men said, "we look like grasshoppers next to the people who live there! We can't take their land."

The Israelites joined in, "Why did God bring us here, only to let these people defeat us? We need a new leader who will take us back to Egypt!"

As the people yelled, Moses and Aaron bowed down at the tent of meeting, the place where the Israelites worshiped God.

Then Joshua and Caleb, two other explorers, stood and said, "If God is happy with us, He will give us this land!"

The people were getting ready to throw stones at them when the glory of God filled the tent. He said to Moses, "After the plagues and the Red Sea, after everything they've seen, they still don't believe!"

"Forgive them," Moses begged. "Show Your mercy and forgive them."

"They are forgiven," God said. "But because they did not believe, they will wander in the wilderness for forty years. Then only Caleb and Joshua will enter Canaan, the land I am giving to My people."

Dear God,

Thank You for wanting the best for us. Please help us always remember Your faithfulness and Your ability to give us Your best. Amen.

Joshua and the Big Wall

(Joshua 6)

We should follow God's instructions,
even when they seem strange. Joshua
and the Israelites did, and they saw
God's mighty power show up!

The Israelites wandered in the wilderness for forty years. Moses died, and Joshua was made the new leader of the Israelites. Once again, the Israelites stood outside the land of Canaan.

The first city in Canaan that they came to was called Jericho. It was surrounded by a huge stone wall, thick and tall and guarded by soldiers.

God told Joshua, "I have given this city to you. But you and all the warriors of Israel must first march around the city one time for six days. The seven priests will carry seven rams' horns as they march in front of the ark of the covenant, where the Ten Commandments are stored. On the seventh day, march around the city seven times. Then have the priests blow a long blast on the rams' horns. When they do, have everyone shout as loud as they can. And the wall of the city will fall down."

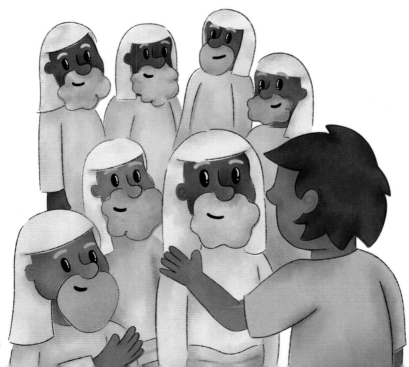

This was not like any battle plan that Joshua had heard before. Joshua didn't know how marching and shouting would knock down a wall. But Joshua knew that God had fought for His people in amazing ways before. So Joshua called the people together and explained God's plan.

On the first day, the Israelites marched around the city, just like God had told them to do. On the second and the third days, they did the same. Then on the fourth, fifth, and sixth days, they marched again.

Even though the Jericho soldiers may have looked at them funny . . . Even though the Israelites were probably getting tired of seeing the same old wall again and again . . . Even though they may have been wondering how in the world what they were doing would knock down a wall . . . they marched.

Then, on the seventh day, they got up early and marched around the city seven times. On the seventh time, the priests blew the horns, and Joshua said, "Shout!"

The Israelites took a deep breath and shouted as loud as they could.

And that wall of Jericho, the huge stone wall, thick and tall, fell to the ground.

Together, with Joshua as their leader, the Israelites finally entered the city of Jericho, the land of Canaan, that God had given to His people.

Dear God,

Thank You for giving us instructions on how to follow You. Help us follow those instructions, even when they seem strange to us. Amen.

Gideon and the Tiny Army

(Judges 6-7)

God wants us to look to Him for help. We can depend on God, just like Gideon did when God called him to do something extraordinary!

Over two hundred years after Joshua crossed into the promised land, a boy named Gideon was born. His life was very difficult because of the Midianites, a group of people who bullied and mistreated the Israelites. Gideon went hungry when the Midianites destroyed the Israelites' crops and stole their cattle. The Israelites called out to God for help.

An angel of the Lord came to Gideon and said, "Mighty hero, the Lord is with you!"

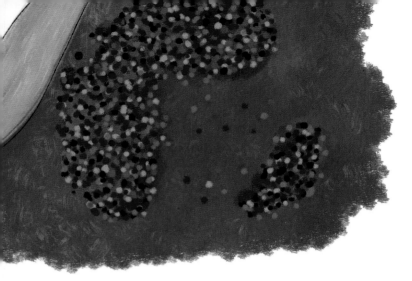

Gideon looked around, confused. "Are you talking to me?" he said. "I'm nobody special."

The angel told him that God had a heroic job for him. God wanted him to defeat the Midianites! Gideon just needed to do what God asked.

Gideon agreed and gathered a huge army of men, but God said, "Your army is way too big! It needs to be smaller."

Usually the bigger the army, the better your chances in battle, but Gideon obeyed God and told his men that whoever was afraid could go home. Most of them did.

But God wanted the army even smaller.

God told Gideon to take his men to the stream. Only the men who cupped the water in their hands should stay. Everyone else could go home.

Gideon did what God asked. Most of the men dipped their faces into the water, but a few cupped the water in their hands.

Gideon and his tiny army stood above the Midianite camp. They spread out, carried torches, and broke a bunch of clay jars to make them look and sound like a big army. Then they watched those Midianites scatter!

In the end, Gideon and just three hundred men defeated the Midianites! Because of this, the Israelites knew God had saved them and that they should always depend on Him.

Dear God,

Thank You that we can always trust You. Help us to always look to You for strength. Amen.

God Calls Samuel

(1 Samuel 1–3)

Did you know that God calls us to do His work? He called Samuel, and Samuel answered Him!

Hundreds of years after the Israelites entered Canaan, Elkanah and his wife Hannah went to the temple every year to worship God.

One year Hannah cried, "Lord, You know that I can't have children. If You gave me a son, I would give him back to You."

Soon after, Hannah and Elkanah had a baby boy, and she remembered her promise to the Lord. When Samuel was old enough, she took him back to the temple where she had first prayed for him.

"The Lord answered my prayer," she told Eli, the priest. "Now we are giving him back to the Lord as I promised."

Eli took Samuel in and taught him how to serve the Lord. Samuel's parents visited him, and his mother made a special robe for him each year. Hannah and Elkanah had five more children. But Samuel grew up serving the Lord.

One night Samuel was in bed in the temple when he heard someone call his name. Samuel ran to Eli. "Here I am. You called me."

"I didn't call you," Eli answered.

"Samuel," the voice called again.

"I'm here!" Samuel said to Eli.

"I didn't call you," Eli said again.

"Samuel."

"I'm here."

"Samuel, I didn't— Ohhh." Eli realized what happened. "If you hear the voice again, say, 'I'm listening, Lord.'"

"Samuel."

"I'm listening, Lord," Samuel answered the voice.

That's when the Lord began to speak to Samuel. He told him all about His plans for Israel.

In the years to come, Samuel would replace Eli as the priest, serving the Lord as He carried out His plans for His people.

Dear God,

Thank You for letting us help, even when we are young. Help us always listen for Your voice so that we may be a part of the plans for Your people. Amen.

David Fights a Giant

(1 Samuel 17)

Even though you might be little,
God can use you in great big ways—
just like He did with David!

When David was a shepherd boy living in Bethlehem, an army of Philistines showed up outside of town to fight the Israelites. The Philistines wanted to make the Israelites their slaves and brought their not-so-secret weapon, a nine-foot-tall giant named Goliath.

"I dare you to send someone for me to fight!" Goliath yelled across the valley. "No one can beat me!"

Most of the Israelites agreed with Goliath. "He's huge!" the soldiers said. "None of us stand a chance!"

Young David, however, thought differently. His father sent him to bring food to his older brothers and the other soldiers. When David saw the giant, he wasn't afraid at all. He protected his family's sheep from wild animals all the time. "Who is this big oaf and why are you putting up with his insults?" he asked.

King Saul heard what David had said to his soldiers and sent for him. Immediately David volunteered, "I'll fight Goliath!"

At first King Saul refused to allow David to go into battle, but David told the king, "The Lord who rescues me from the claws of lions and bears will also rescue me from Goliath!"

So Saul gave David permission to fight the giant. He even offered to let David use his royal armor. But David knew he could fight better without it.

David went down to a nearby river and gathered five smooth stones for the sling he used to protect his sheep.

When David showed up to fight with his sling and shepherd's staff, Goliath laughed. "Am I a dog, that you come at me with a stick?"

"You come at me with a sword and a spear, but I come at you in the name of the God of Israel!" David answered.

As Goliath ran to attack him, David quickly placed a stone in his sling, spun it around in fast circles, then released it toward the oncoming giant. *Wham!* The rock hit Goliath right between the eyes and down he went!

"David won!" the Israelite soldiers cheered as the Philistine army ran away in fear.

Dear God,

Thank You that You can use us to do big things for You! Amen.

Jonathan Helps His Best Friend

(1 Samuel 18, 20)

Do you have a best friend? God gives
us friends to help each other, like
Jonathan helped David.

David and Jonathan were best friends.

But there was a problem. King Saul, Jonathan's father, was very jealous of David.

Why?

After he defeated Goliath, David went on to win many more battles and became famous among the Israelites. King Saul had been disobeying God, and God had rejected him as king. Saul began to worry that his people would want to make David their king instead, so he secretly planned to kill David.

David found out about King Saul's plans and asked his friend Jonathan for help.

"Why would my father want to kill you?" Jonathan asked David. "You haven't done anything wrong!"

David came up with a plan.

The next day, a big festival was being held. David told Jonathan, "If King Saul gets angry that I'm not there, you'll see that what I'm telling you is true."

And guess what? It was true. King Saul had planned on killing David at the party, and he got very angry when he found out David wouldn't be there. Jonathan knew he must help his best friend get away from his father.

The next morning Jonathan went out to a field and shot an arrow past the stone where David was hiding. Jonathan motioned to his servant, who ran out to retrieve the arrow, and yelled, "The arrow is still ahead of you!"

This was a signal to David that he was right, that Saul did want to kill him. Jonathan was telling David that he must run away.

Jonathan knew that God wanted David to be the next king, and they promised their families would always be loyal to each other. Though they were both very sad to say goodbye, Jonathan had saved his best friend's life.

Dear God,

Thank You for giving us good friends. Please help us be a great friend like Jonathan was to David. Amen.

A King After God's Own Heart

(1 Samuel 16; 2 Samuel 2)

Ever since David was a little boy, God had a plan for him. Do you know that God has a plan for your life too?

God wanted a new king for Israel. He told his prophet Samuel to travel to Bethlehem and meet with a man named Jesse and his eight boys. God said He would choose a new king from Jesse's sons.

At first, Samuel thought God's choice must be the oldest son, Eliab. He was tall and strong and looked like a king. But God told Samuel, "I don't see things the way you see them. People judge others by the way they look, but I see their hearts."

God's choice was actually Jesse's youngest son, David. It was David who would one day be king.

God was with David, and he went on to defeat Goliath, play music for King Saul, and lead the Israelites' army. David was so good at his job and became so popular among the people that King Saul became very jealous and tried to kill David. So David went into hiding.

But God never forgot David or the plans that He had for him.

One day David heard that King Saul and three of his four sons, including David's best friend, Jonathan, had been killed in a battle. David was very sad that his friend had died, but God told him that it was time for him to become king.

David became king of the southern kingdom of Judah.

Later, after many battles with the northern kingdom and the death of Saul's last son, Ishbosheth, David became king of all of Israel—just like God had planned!

Dear God,

Thank You that You have a plan for our life. And thank You that Jesus would one day come to be the King for the whole world. Amen.

The Wise King

(1 Kings 3)

If you could have anything you wanted, what would you wish for? Choose wisely!

King David ruled Israel for forty years. Just before he died, he made his son Solomon king.

One night God spoke to Solomon in a dream. God asked him, "What do you want? Ask, and I will give it to you."

Did Solomon ask for more money or power? Maybe a longer life or a cool new toy? Nope! Solomon asked God for wisdom. He wanted God to give him an understanding heart. He wanted to be able to tell the difference between right and wrong so he could be a better king and better serve God and His people.

This request made God very happy. Not only did God give Solomon wisdom, but God also gave him what he did not ask for—riches and fame!

One day two women came to Solomon to solve a problem. They were arguing over a baby. One woman said the baby was hers. The other said she was the real mother of the child. Only one of them was telling the truth. How could Solomon tell who was being honest?

He asked a guard for a sword. "It's only fair that you each get half of the baby."

"Sounds fair," one woman answered.

"No! Give her the child. Please do not kill him!" the other cried.

Solomon knew immediately who the real mother was and gave the child to the woman who wanted the baby to live.

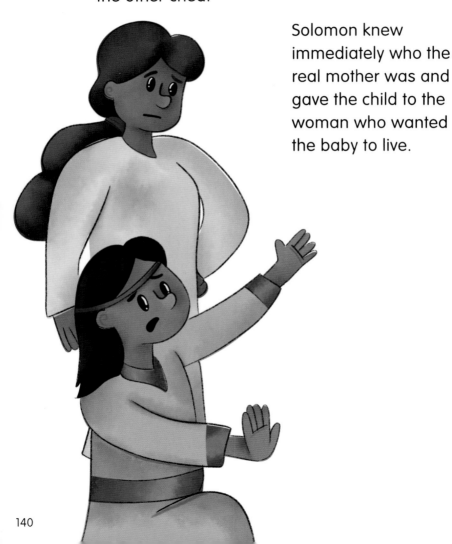

The people were amazed when they saw the wisdom that God had given Solomon.

Dear God,

Please give us wisdom and an understanding heart to tell the difference between right and wrong. Amen.

The One True God

(1 Kings 18)

God is the only one we should ever worship. Nothing is more powerful than Him!

God's first commandment to Moses and the Israelites was to have no other gods before Him. This meant that God wanted His people to worship only Him, the one true God.

Sixty years after wise King Solomon, the new king of Israel, Ahab, was worshiping a god named Baal. Because of this, God punished Israel by not allowing it to rain. The crops dried up, and everyone was very thirsty.

God sent the prophet Elijah, whose name means "My God is the Lord," to prove to Ahab that the Lord is God, not Baal.

Elijah told Ahab he needed to make a choice. "If the Lord is God, follow Him. But if Baal is God, then follow Him." Elijah then challenged Ahab to a competition: the Lord versus Baal! Elijah would call to the Lord, and Ahab's 450 men would call to Baal. "The god who answers with fire is the true God," Elijah said. Ahab agreed to the contest.

Ahab and his men went first. They built an altar to Baal and stacked it with firewood and then put a bull they had killed on top. Ahab's 450 men called on the name of Baal from morning until noon, shouting and dancing around the altar. Nothing happened.

"Baal can't hear you," Elijah joked. "Maybe he's taking a nap or going to the bathroom?"

Then Elijah prepared another altar, also stacking it with firewood and a dead bull. And to take it up a notch, he completely soaked it in water.

When Elijah called out to the Lord, fire immediately flashed down from heaven and completely burned up the altar!

When all the people saw this, including Ahab, they fell down on the ground with their faces in the dirt and cried out, "The Lord—He is the one true God! Yes, the Lord is God!"

God then sent a great rainstorm and ended the drought.

Dear God,

Thank You that You are the one true and only God! Thank You for loving us. Please help us remember that You are more powerful than anyone or anything! Amen.

Elisha, the Prophet's Apprentice

(1 Kings 19; 2 Kings 2, 4)

Did you know that God gives us all we need to live and work for Him?

Elisha, whose name means "God is salvation," was the prophet Elijah's assistant. When Elijah was finished with the work that God had for him, it was time for Elisha to take over his job.

The two prophets crossed east over the Jordan River. Suddenly, a chariot of fire came down from the sky, drawn by a horse of fire! Elijah's cloak fell to the ground as he climbed into the chariot. Then he was carried up into heaven.

Bye, Elijah!

Elisha picked up the cloak and crossed back over the river. He was now the new prophet in town.

Elisha went on to perform many miracles. When the town of Jericho did not have safe water to drink, Elisha went to the spring where the people drew their water. He poured in a bowl of salt and announced, "This is what the Lord says: 'I have purified this water!'" And the water was clean.

Another time Elisha helped a poor widow and her two sons. All they owned that was worth any money was one small flask of olive oil.

Elisha told the boys to borrow as many empty jars as they could from their neighbors. Elisha then told the widow to pour oil from the one small flask into the larger jars until they were full.

In the end, she had so much oil to sell that they were no longer poor.

One day Elisha met a kind woman who had always wanted children, but she couldn't have a baby. Elisha told her that she would have a son in one year, and she did.

When the boy got older, he suddenly fell sick and died. Elisha came back and prayed over the body. God brought the boy back to life!

Dear God,

Thank You for loving and helping us. Please give us the strength to love and help others. Amen.

The Girl Who Saved Her People

(Esther 1-10)

You are no accident. God has put you at the right place at the right time!

After the time of Elijah and Elisha, the Israelites were ruled by a Persian king named Xerxes. Xerxes was very rich and powerful and was always used to getting his way. When his wife, Queen Vashti, wouldn't do what he wanted her to do, he got angry and kicked her out of his palace.

King Xerxes then held a contest to find a new queen. Young women from all over the kingdom, including a beautiful Israelite girl who lived in Persia named Esther, were brought to the palace. When King Xerxes saw Esther, he immediately chose her to be the new queen.

It was God's plan for Esther to be the queen for a very important reason.

One of the king's evil advisors, Haman, was plotting to kill all the Jews. But no one knew Esther was Jewish.

Esther's cousin Mordecai came to her for help when he found out what Haman wanted to do. She must tell the king about Haman's plan and save her people!

"Perhaps God has made you queen for such a time as this?" Mordecai said.

Coming to see the king of Persia without being invited was a very dangerous thing to do—even for a queen. But Esther bravely went to the king and asked both Xerxes and Haman to dinner.

Thankfully, the king was pleased to see Esther, and he accepted her invitation.

After dinner, Esther told King Xerxes, "Haman is planning on killing all the Jews, which means he wants me dead too!" Haman was shocked, and the king was furious. Xerxes ordered that Haman be taken away and punished.

King Xerxes then gave Haman's old job to Mordecai.

God had chosen Esther to be at the right place at the right time. Esther acted bravely and saved her people!

Dear God,

Thank You for choosing us for Your special purposes. Please help us follow You. Amen.

Three Friends in the Hot Seat

(Daniel 3)

Never be afraid to stand up for God. He is always with you, just like He was with Shadrach, Meshach, and Abednego!

Just before the time of Esther, the Israelites were ruled by the Babylonian king Nebuchadnezzar, who ordered that a ninety-foot gold statue be made to look just like him. He then demanded that everybody fall down and worship the statue. Anyone who didn't would be thrown into the fiery furnace.

But the second commandment that God gave to Moses is to not serve or bow down to idols. So Shadrach, Meshach, and Abednego, three Israelites who lived in Babylon, knew they couldn't worship anything other than God.

Some men came to the king to complain. "There are three men who refuse to bow down to your statue."

The king was angry. "How dare they! Bring them to me!"

Shadrach, Meshach, and Abednego were brought before the king.

King Nebuchadnezzar warned them, "If you don't bow down to my statue, I will throw you in the fiery furnace!"

"Even if you do, there is no way we're worshiping a statue of you," they said. "We worship only God, just has He commanded!"

The king became furious. "Throw them in the furnace!" he yelled.

The furnace was so hot that it killed the guards who threw them in.

But God protected Shadrach, Meshach, and Abednego!

King Nebuchadnezzar looked into the flames and saw four men, not three!

Shadrach, Meshach, and Abednego walked out of the furnace completely unharmed. They didn't even smell like smoke!

"Praise be to the God of Shadrach, Meshach, and Abednego!" Nebuchadnezzar said. "He has sent His angel and rescued His servants!"

Dear God,

We know that You will always be with us and that You can protect us in any situation. Please help us always stand up for You! Amen.

Daniel and the Friendly Lions

(Daniel 6)

Lions may be the Kings of the jungle,
but God is the King of kings!

Daniel was another Israelite living in Babylon. He was friends with Shadrach, Meshach, and Abednego. King Nebuchadnezzar gave the four friends important jobs in the kingdom.

Daniel was so good at his job that even after the Babylonians were conquered, the new king, Darius, planned to give Daniel the most important job in the kingdom. This made King Darius's other advisors very jealous.

"He's not even one of us," they complained. "We have to find a way to get rid of Daniel."

They came up with a plan. The king's advisors knew that Daniel prayed only to God. So they tricked the king into signing a law that for the next thirty days, no one could pray to anyone except King Darius. If they did, they would be thrown into the lions' den!

But Daniel knew the law was wrong,
and he kept praying to God.

The advisors' plan had worked. They went straight to the king and told him what Daniel had done. King Darius was very upset, but he had to follow his own law. So he ordered that Daniel be thrown into the lions' den.

But the king liked Daniel so much that he hoped Daniel's God would protect him.

The next day King Darius rushed to the lions' den to check on Daniel. "Daniel!" he called out. "Are you okay?"

"I'm fine!" Daniel answered. "God protected me. He sent an angel and shut the lions' mouths."

King Darius was so happy that God saved Daniel, but he was furious that his advisors had tricked him into signing the law. He ordered that they be thrown to the hungry lions!

Dear God,

Thank You that You are stronger and more powerful than anything we might be afraid of. Thank You for loving and taking care of Your children. Amen.

Jonah and the Great Fish

(Jonah 1-4)

No matter what we do, God always has compassion on us when we turn to Him.

Like Elijah and Elisha, Jonah was a prophet. God wanted Jonah to travel over five hundred miles to preach to the people of the great city of Nineveh. He wanted Jonah to tell the people that if they did not stop doing bad things, God would destroy their city.

But as soon as Jonah heard God's instructions, he ran in the opposite direction!

The people of Nineveh were the enemies of the people of Israel. Jonah thought that if he didn't deliver God's message, God would destroy the Ninevites and that would be a great thing for Israel.

So Jonah boarded a ship bound for Tarshish, which was over two thousand miles away from Nineveh.

But God sent a great storm. It was so strong that the boat started to sink.

Jonah told the sailors that God had sent the storm because he was running from Him. Jonah told them that if they threw him overboard, God would stop the storm.

The sailors threw Jonah over the side of the ship, and the storm immediately stopped.

As Jonah sank under the waves, God sent a big fish to swallow Jonah whole!

Inside the fish, Jonah prayed and thanked God for saving him.

Three days later, the fish spat Jonah up on dry land. Jonah decided to follow God's plan now and headed to Nineveh.

Once he arrived in the city, Jonah preached God's message to the people. He warned them to turn away from their evil ways and to follow God. And they listened!

They said they were sorry for what they had done and asked God not to punish them. And God took pity on the people of Nineveh and did not destroy their city.

Dear God,

Thank You for always being with us even if we try to run from You like Jonah did. Thank You for loving us, and please help us always love and forgive others. Amen.

NEW
TESTAMENT

Gabriel Visits Mary and Joseph

(Luke 1:26-38; Matthew 1:18-25)

God chose Mary and Joseph to help with
His plan—to save us and be with us
in a whole new way.

Many years after Abraham and Jacob and
David lived, a man named Joseph, who was
from that same family line, lived in Nazareth.
He was planning to marry a girl named Mary.

One day the angel Gabriel visited Mary and said, "God is pleased with you!"

Mary stared at him wide-eyed.

"Don't be afraid," he said. "God has chosen you to give birth to His son. You will name Him Jesus, and He will reign forever over an endless kingdom."

"How can this be?" Mary asked. "I'm not even married yet."

"Nothing is impossible with God," Gabriel explained.

"I serve the Lord," Mary answered. "Let it happen just as you said."

When Joseph found out that Mary was going to have a baby before they were married, he was upset. But Gabriel visited Joseph in a dream and explained everything.

"Joseph," he said, "don't be afraid to take Mary as your wife. The child she is carrying is God's own Son. You will name Him Jesus. And He will save the people from their sins."

Joseph woke up and ran to Mary. He did just as Gabriel said and took Mary as his wife. And together, they waited for Jesus, the Son of God, to be born.

Therefore the LORD Himself will give you a sign: Behold, a virgin will be with child and bear a son, and she will call His name Immanuel.

Isaiah 7:14

Dear God,

Thank You for choosing Mary to be a part of Your most important plan. Help us be like Mary, always willing to say yes to You. Amen.

God with Us

(Matthew 1:25; Luke 2:1-20)

Did you know that God is always with us? Long ago, He sent His Son to be with His people here on earth.

The ruler of Rome, Caesar Augustus, told the people, "You have to go back to your hometown. We want to count your family."

Joseph was from Bethlehem, so he and his wife, Mary, had to go there. But Mary was going to have a baby very soon.

Joseph gently helped her onto their donkey. Then they traveled from Galilee down the hills and around the curves to Bethlehem.

There were no rooms available for Joseph and Mary to stay in. So they stayed in a place where the animals were kept, and the baby Jesus was born.

That night, in the fields near Bethlehem, there was a burst of light in the sky, then an angel appeared. The shepherds below were terrified.

The angel said, "Don't be afraid! I have good news! Your Savior was born in Bethlehem tonight! He is Christ the Lord."

The Jews had been expecting the Savior for a very long time. Was He finally here?

The angel said, "You will find Him wrapped in cloth, lying in a feeding box."

Then more angels burst from the sky. They shouted joyfully, "Glory to God! Peace on earth!"

195

After the angels disappeared, the shepherds ran into Bethlehem.

Suddenly, they stopped. They saw a baby wrapped in cloth, lying in a feeding box. The shepherds looked at Him, amazed, and told Mary and Joseph everything the angels had said.

Mary looked at this baby, thinking about everything that had happened.

He was Jesus, Immanuel, "God with us."

Dear God,

Thank You for sending Your Son to be with us. Help us know how important that gift is. And help us follow You like Mary, Joseph, and the shepherds did. Amen.

Jerusalem

Wise Men Worship Jesus

(Matthew 2:1-12)

Did you know that God invites us to
worship Him? He invited the wise men,
and He invites us too!

Bethlehem

198

After Jesus was born, wise men who studied planets and stars came from the east to Jerusalem. They were asking people where they could find the newborn King of the Jews.

"We saw His star in the east, and we have followed it here," they explained. "We want to worship Him."

Persia

The mean King Herod heard about it and was upset. He was afraid that this new ruler, the one the prophets had written about, would replace him. King Herod asked his priests, "Where did the prophets say the Messiah, the Savior, would be born?"

"He will be born in Bethlehem," they answered.

Bethlehem was not very far from Jerusalem. If this new ruler had been born there, King Herod wanted to find him. King Herod called the wise men to him. "When you find the child, please let me know so that I can go worship Him too."

The wise men kept following that bright star until it stopped over a house in Bethlehem. Inside that house they saw Jesus and His mother, Mary.

These wise men from far away had finally found what they had been searching for. They were so happy. Immediately they bowed down and worshiped Jesus. To honor Him, they gave Him the gifts of frankincense and myrrh, which were valuable spices, and gold.

Before they left, God warned the wise men in a dream not to go back and tell King Herod where Jesus was. They went home a different way instead, filled with joy for having found the newborn King.

Dear Jesus,

Thank You for coming to Earth. Please help us always find a way to worship You. Amen.

Jesus in His Father's House

(Luke 2:41-50)

Jesus, the Son of God, loved to learn
in His Father's house. He showed us
how important it is to spend time
learning about God.

When Jesus was twelve years old, He went with His parents, Mary and Joseph, to the Passover Feast in Jerusalem. The feast was a time to remember and celebrate God helping the Israelites escape from Pharaoh in Egypt many years ago.

Jesus and His parents went to the feast every year. The streets were full of people and food.

They worshiped and celebrated as they had always done. Then they packed up and started walking the long journey home.

Many families walked together out of Jerusalem as they left the celebration. Mary and Joseph thought that Jesus was somewhere in the group. But after a while, they realized that they hadn't seen Jesus for some time.

They began asking among their friends and family, but no one had seen Jesus.

Starting to worry, they turned around and began walking back to Jerusalem, trying to find Jesus the whole way. By the time they got to Jerusalem, they were very worried. They began looking all through the city.

After three long days of searching for Jesus, they found Him. There He was, sitting in the temple with all of the teachers, listening and asking questions.

Mary asked Jesus, "Why did You do this? We have been looking for You everywhere!"

Jesus looked up at His parents. "Didn't you know that I would be in My Father's house?"

Mary and Joseph were happy to have found Jesus. Together, the three of them walked home.

Jesus continued to spend time with His Father and continued to grow in wisdom and faith.

Dear Jesus,

Thank You for reminding us how important it is to spend time in God's house. Help us always be willing to listen and ask questions just like You did. Amen.

Jesus Is Baptized

(Luke 1; Matthew 3; John 1)

John helped prepare the people to meet Jesus. He showed us how to be bold in telling others about Him.

A few months before Gabriel visited Mary and Joseph, Mary's cousin Elizabeth received some surprising news too.

Even though Elizabeth and her husband, Zechariah, were too old to have children, an angel told Zechariah that they were going to have a baby boy. The angel said to name him John. The angel told him that John would one day prepare people for Jesus, just as the prophet Isaiah had said long ago.

When John grew up, he began preaching about Jesus. He was a little wild-looking, with clothes made of camel's hair, and he ate locusts and honey. But the people listened to him.

John taught the people to ask for forgiveness for the things they did wrong, and he baptized them in the Jordan River. People came from all around to hear John preach and to be baptized by him.

"Who are you to be baptizing people?" some leaders of the church asked.

"I am baptizing with water," John answered. "But there is One who is coming, and I am not even worthy to untie His sandals. He will baptize you with the Holy Spirit."

The very next day Jesus came down to the Jordan River to be baptized by John. John knew exactly who Jesus was: the Messiah, God's own Son.

John said, "No, Jesus. You shouldn't be baptized by me. I should be baptized by You!"

"Please, John, this is the right way," Jesus said. "This is the way it should be done."

So John did as Jesus said,
and he baptized Him.

As Jesus rose from the water, the heavens opened, and the Spirit of God landed on Jesus like a dove. A voice from heaven said, "This is My Son, and I am so pleased with Him."

Dear Jesus,

Please show us how to be like John and prepare others for meeting You. Help us obey and follow the path that God has for our life. Amen.

Jesus Stands Up to Evil

(Matthew 4:1-11)

Jesus showed us how to use God's Word to stand up to evil. We can still use the power of God's Word just like Jesus did.

After Jesus was baptized, the Holy Spirit led Him into the wilderness. Jesus was going to be tested there. For forty days, He stayed in the wilderness and fasted, not eating anything. He was very, very hungry.

That's when the devil came to see Jesus. "So, I hear that You're the Son of God," he said. "If that's true, why don't You just turn these rocks into bread?"

"The Scriptures say that a person doesn't live only by bread," Jesus answered. "A person lives by what the Lord says."

So the devil tried again. This time he took Jesus to the city of Jerusalem and put Him on the very top of the temple.

"If You really are the Son of God, jump off. You won't get hurt," the devil said. "The Scriptures say that God's angels are watching over You. They will catch You."

"The Scriptures also say not to test God,"
Jesus answered.

So then the devil took Jesus to the top of a mountain. From there, Jesus could see all of the kingdoms and all of the riches of the world.

"All You have to do is worship me," the devil said. "Then You can have all of this."

"Go away, Satan!" Jesus said. "The Scriptures say that a person must only worship God!"

Seeing that Jesus wouldn't give in to temptation, Satan left Him alone, at least for a little while.

After that, angels came to Jesus in the wilderness and helped Him.

Dear Jesus,

Thank You for showing us how to deal with the devil. Help us know what the Bible says about him so that we can stay strong whenever he comes our way. Amen.

The Disciples Follow Jesus

(Luke 5:1-11, 27-28; 6:12-16;

Matthew 9:9; John 1:35-50)

The disciples dropped everything to follow Jesus. They showed us how to respond when Jesus calls us to follow Him.

After His time in the wilderness, Jesus began teaching and preaching to the people in Galilee. One day He was by the Sea of Galilee when a large crowd formed.

He stepped into a boat on the shore and asked the fishermen, Simon and Andrew, to pull the boat out into the water so that the crowd could see Him better. So they did.

When Jesus was finished speaking, He told Simon, "Let's go out a little farther and catch some fish."

"We fished all night long and didn't catch a thing," Simon said. "But if You say so . . ." Simon and Andrew slowly dropped the net into the water.

First, they felt a little tug. Then the boat started to lean a little. And before long, the net started to rip from all of the fish that they had caught.

"Hey! Come help us!" Simon and Andrew yelled to their friends James and John, who were in a nearby boat.

James and John came to help, but then both boats were sinking from the weight of the fish! They all looked to Jesus, amazed.

"Follow Me," Jesus said, "and I'll show you how to fish for people."

And with that, Simon, Andrew, James, and John left their boats behind to follow Jesus.

Jesus continued to travel and preach. One day He saw a man named Philip and said, "Follow Me." So Philip followed Him.

As they continued to travel, they met a man named Matthew collecting taxes from the people. Jesus went over to the man and said, "Come and follow Me." Matthew stood up, left his booth, and went with Jesus and the others.

After Jesus had preached a while longer in that area, He went off by Himself to a mountain to pray. He talked to God all night.

And in the morning, Jesus told twelve of His followers that He had chosen them to be His disciples.

Those twelve men were Simon Peter, James and John, Andrew, Philip, Bartholomew, Matthew, Thomas, another James, Thaddaeus, Simon, and Judas Iscariot. The twelve disciples stayed with Jesus, traveling with Him, learning from Him, and preaching the message of Jesus.

Dear Jesus,

Thank You for calling all of us to follow You. Help us listen to You and learn from You. And help us to put following You first. Amen.

One Man Thanks Jesus

(Luke 17:11-19)

Did you know that Jesus wants us to be thankful? The leper was thankful, even when no one else was.

One day Jesus entered a village on His way to Jerusalem. He saw ten men standing in the distance. These men were lepers. They could not come close to other people because they

had a skin disease that other people could catch. They usually had to stay away from their families and friends outside the village until they got better. But many times, they never got better.

The men had heard about Jesus and His power to heal people. They called out, "Jesus! Help us, please!"

Jesus told them, "Go now, and show the priests that your disease is gone."

Their skin wasn't better yet, but the ten men turned and started walking toward the priests, just as Jesus had told them to do. And while they were walking, suddenly their skin was healed! There was no redness, no sores—just clear, healthy skin.

231

One man stared at his skin for a moment. Then immediately he turned back and ran toward Jesus. When he reached Him, the man fell down at Jesus's feet, thanking Him.

Jesus looked into the distance. "But weren't there ten men who were healed? Where are the other nine?" Jesus said. "You were the only one to give glory to God. Now go, your faith has healed you."

Dear Jesus,

Thank You for the many blessings we have in our lives. Help us always be thankful and give God the glory for those blessings. Amen.

The Sermon on the Mount

(Matthew 5-7)

Once Jesus's ministry began,
He was always teaching and
preaching to the people.
They learned so much from
Him about God's kingdom.

One day when Jesus was in Galilee, there was a crowd following Him, as there often was. So Jesus walked to the mountain and sat down and told them all about God and His kingdom.

"Those who are sad will be comforted. Those who seek what is right will find it. Those who give mercy will get mercy," Jesus taught them.

"The pure in heart will see God, and the peacemakers will be called children of God. When people make fun of you or are mean to you because of Me," Jesus told them, "be glad, because you will be rewarded."

Jesus told the people how they were the salt of the earth and the light of the world, how they should let the light of God within them shine so that it would glorify God.

Then He taught about God's law and how He came to make it come true. He taught that those who keep the law will be called great in heaven.

237

He taught that people should give to the poor and to do it quietly. He taught them how to pray to God with all their hearts, asking only for what they need each day, forgiving others as God forgives them.

He taught them not to worry but to depend on God to give them what they needed, just as He clothes the flowers and feeds the birds.

He taught them not to judge others but to treat others just as they wanted to be treated.

And when Jesus finished speaking and preaching, the people looked at each other amazed. They had never heard someone preach like that before.

Jesus was more than someone who studied the Word of God. He was the living Word of God.

Dear Jesus,

Thank You for teaching us and showing us the way to God's kingdom. Help us to pray and give and love like You do. Amen.

Jesus Feeds Five Thousand

(John 6:1-14)

Do you trust God to do big things
with your little offerings? Jesus did!
And we can too!

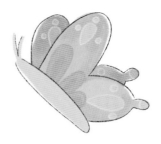

Jesus was on a mountain with His disciples when He saw a crowd following them.

It was getting late, and it was time to eat, so Jesus asked Philip, "Where can we buy bread for all of these people?" Of course, Jesus already knew what He was going to do.

Philip laughed. "We'd have to work for a year just to buy a crumb of bread for everybody!"

Just then Andrew walked up. "There's a boy who has five loaves of bread and two fish," he said. Then he looked out at all the people. "But that wouldn't go very far in this crowd."

Jesus just smiled and said, "Tell everyone to sit down to eat."

And they all did—thousands of them.

Jesus took the loaves of bread, thanked God for them, and told the disciples to hand them out to the people.

He did the same thing with the fish. The disciples knew there wasn't enough for everyone, but they did what Jesus said anyway.

No matter how much bread they handed out, no matter how many people they saw, the disciples still didn't run out of food. Everyone ate until they were full.

When the people finished eating, Jesus said, "Now go around and collect the extra food so that we don't waste anything."

So the disciples did. And to their amazement, even after those five loaves and two fish fed thousands of people, there were still twelve baskets of food left over!

> Dear Jesus,
>
> Thank You for showing us how to trust God for what we need. Help us always remember what God can do even with our tiniest offerings. Amen.

Above the Waves

(Matthew 14:22-33; Mark 6:45-52; John 6:16-21)

Do you know that you can trust Jesus?
He will always be there for you!

After Jesus miraculously fed a huge crowd
of people with just five loaves of bread and
two fish, He asked His twelve disciples to row
across the Sea of Galilee and meet Him later
on the other side.

Jesus then went up a mountain by Himself to
pray. He knew how important it was to spend
time with God.

While Jesus was praying, a big storm rolled over the sea. Lightning flashed, and huge waves crashed against the disciples' boat. Jesus saw that His friends were in trouble and went to help them.

But Jesus did not go
to them in a boat . . .
He walked out to
them on the water!

When the disciples saw Him walking
toward them, they were terrified! They
thought they were seeing a ghost.

"Don't be afraid! It's Me!" Jesus said.

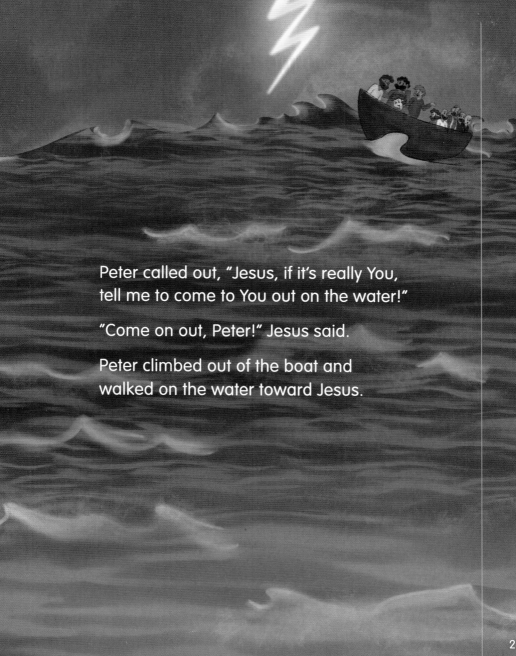

Peter called out, "Jesus, if it's really You,
tell me to come to You out on the water!"

"Come on out, Peter!" Jesus said.

Peter climbed out of the boat and
walked on the water toward Jesus.

But Peter took his eyes off of Jesus and looked at the waves and the rain.

He started to sink!

"Help me! I'm afraid!" Peter pleaded.

Right away, Jesus reached out and caught him.

"Why didn't you trust in Me?" Jesus asked as He pulled Peter up out of the water.

When Jesus and Peter stepped into the boat, the storm immediately stopped.

The disciples were amazed and worshiped Jesus. They all realized that He must be the Son of God!

Dear Jesus,

You are more powerful than the wind and the waves! Thank You for helping us and saving us. Help us always put our trust in You. Amen.

Who Is Your Neighbor?

(Luke 10:25–37)

Jesus showed us how to treat our neighbors—
even when they are very different from us.

One day a man asked Jesus how he could go to heaven.

"Love God and love your neighbor," Jesus replied.

"My neighbor?" the man asked. "Who is that?"

Jesus answered the man's question with a story.

"A man was traveling from Jerusalem to Jericho," Jesus said. This was a long and difficult eighteen-mile hike through a very dry and rocky desert with lots of hills.

"Suddenly, he was attacked by robbers! They beat him up, took everything he had, and ran away. The man lay on the side of the trail alone, almost dead."

"A little later, a priest came down the road," Jesus continued.

A priest was someone who was supposed to help people and teach them about God. But did the priest stop to help?

Nope.

"The priest saw the injured man, but he passed right by him."

"Soon a Levite came by," Jesus said.

Levites were officials who served in God's temple. He should have helped too, but did he?

Nope.

"The Levite stepped to the other side of the trail and walked past him."

"But then a Samaritan came along," Jesus said.

Samaritans were considered enemies of the people who lived around Jerusalem. So did the Samaritan stop to help?

Yes!

"When the Samaritan saw the injured man, he felt sorry for him. The Samaritan bandaged his wounds, brought him to an inn, and took care of him.

"Then the Samaritan paid the innkeeper to keep caring for the man until he was better."

Jesus asked the man he was telling the story to, "Which of the three do you think was a neighbor to the man attacked by the robbers?"

What do you think?

Dear God,

Please help us always to be a good neighbor to everyone, no matter where they live, what language they speak, or what they look like. Amen.

Sibling Rivalry

(Luke 10:38-42)

Do you know that loving Jesus is the most important thing you can do?

Mary and Martha were sisters who lived in a small town near Jerusalem.

One day Jesus visited their town, and the sisters invited Him to their house.

Jesus accepted their invitation and Martha got to work.

While Martha was busy serving all their guests and preparing dinner, Mary sat at Jesus's feet, listening to Him teach.

This upset Martha.

Martha went to Jesus. She knew Mary would do what Jesus said.

"Can You please tell Mary to help me?" Martha asked. "I'm doing all the work while she just sits there."

"My dear Martha," Jesus said with a smile. "You are worried and upset about all these details. But there is only one thing you really need. And your sister, Mary, knows what that is!"

Mary knew that having the chance to sit with Jesus and listen to Him was more important than anything else she could do.

Dear Jesus,

Thank You for loving us and always being with us. Please help us love You more by spending time with You in prayer. Amen.

The Wind and the Waves Obey Him

(Matthew 8:23-27; Mark 4:35-41; Luke 8:22-25)

Did you know that God is in control of everything? Even the weather obeys Him!

Jesus performed many miracles. He turned water into wine, healed the sick, and even helped His friends catch fish! But His disciples were amazed by what happened next at the Sea of Galilee.

Crowds of people had been following Jesus and listening to His teachings. When night fell, Jesus said to His disciples, "Let's go to the other side of the sea."

The disciples all got into a boat with Jesus, and there were other boats on the water as well.

As they crossed, a huge thunderstorm with powerful rain and winds blew over the sea. Big, angry waves tossed the boats about.

They were going to sink!

But Jesus wasn't worried. In fact, He was sleeping in the back of one of the boats!

"Jesus! Wake up!" the disciples yelled. "Don't You care that we are going to drown?"

Jesus opened His eyes and sat up.

He looked out over the water and shouted to the wind and waves, "Silence! Be still!"

Right away, the wind slowed. The waves died down. The thunder and lightning and rain stopped.

Everything was perfectly calm.

The disciples were terrified and could hardly believe their eyes. They turned to each other and asked, "Who is this man? Even the wind and the waves obey Him!"

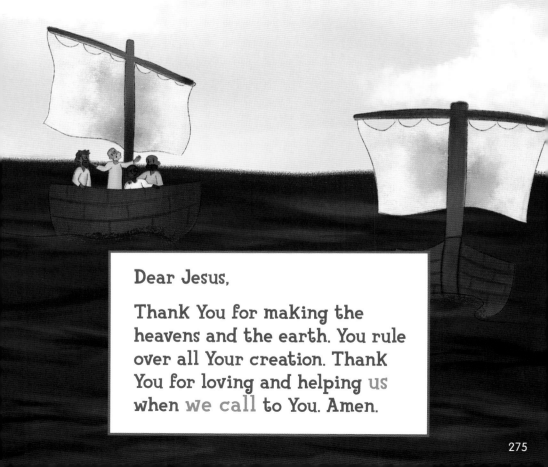

Dear Jesus,

Thank You for making the heavens and the earth. You rule over all Your creation. Thank You for loving and helping us when we call to You. Amen.

The Great Healer

(Matthew 9:18-26; Mark 5:21-43; Luke 8:40-56)

Do you know that God answers your prayers? One day Jesus answered the prayers of two different people in amazing ways.

People followed Jesus everywhere He went.

When He sailed across the Sea of Galilee with the disciples, a large crowd gathered on the shore to greet them.

A religious leader named Jairus fell to his knees at Jesus's feet and cried out, "Jesus! Please help my little girl! She is very sick. Please come to my house and heal her."

Jesus felt compassion for Jairus and agreed to follow him home.

As they made their way through the crowd, a woman who had been sick for a very long time reached out toward Jesus. "If only I can touch Him, then I will be healed," she prayed.

As soon as she touched Jesus's clothes, she didn't feel sick anymore.

Jesus turned and told her, "Dear woman, the faith you have in Me has healed you."

When Jesus reached Jairus's house, they were told some bad news.

"Your daughter is dead," a man said to Jairus. "There is no need for Jesus now."

But Jesus told Jairus, "Don't be afraid. Have faith. Your little girl is not dead. She is only sleeping."

Jairus's neighbors thought that was ridiculous. "Of course she's dead," they said.

Jesus went inside to the girl and took her hand.
He then said to her, "Little girl, get up!"

Right away, the girl sat up. Then she stood up and started walking around.

Everyone was amazed. Jesus had healed Jairus's daughter!

Dear Jesus,

Thank You that You can heal the sick. Please give us the faith to know that You can do anything. Amen.

Let Them Come!

(Matthew 19:14; Mark 10:13-15)

Did you know that Jesus loves every single person, no matter how tall or how small?

Jesus's disciples were very important to Him.

He told them things that He didn't tell others.
He let them see His most powerful miracles.
And they were the first to know that He
was the Son of God.

When parents began to bring their children to Jesus to be blessed, the disciples told the moms and dads that Jesus had more important things to do and couldn't be bothered with a bunch of kids.

This upset Jesus. He loved everyone—no matter how tall or small. He said, "Let the

children come to Me. Don't keep them away! The kingdom of God belongs to those who are like these little children."

Jesus had taught earlier that the kingdom of God belonged to those who were humble, who had pure hearts, and who realized their need for Him—just like these children!

The disciples knew they had made a mistake.
They stepped back to let the children come to
Jesus.

Jesus welcomed the
children with open
arms and prayed for
them, just like their
parents had asked.

Dear Jesus,

Thank You for loving everyone, no matter how tall or how small—including us! Help us always remember how much we need You. Amen.

The Widow's Offering

(Mark 12:38-44; Luke 21:1-4)

Do you know that God wants us to trust Him with everything?

Jesus had become famous because of His teaching and miracles. When He arrived in Jerusalem, the people welcomed Him like a king.

He visited God's temple there and told the religious leaders that it was more important to love God than it was to follow rules they had made up.

This upset the leaders, but they were afraid to arrest Jesus because of how popular He had become.

One of the rules the leaders followed was to donate part of the money they earned to the temple.

One day Jesus was watching people put their money into the temple offering boxes. He saw a rich man throw in a big sack of money.

The man probably hoped everyone would think, *Look at all the money he gave. What an important guy who follows the rules.*

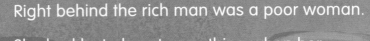

Right behind the rich man was a poor woman.

She had lost almost everything when her husband died. In fact, all she had were two tiny coins worth less than a penny.

She put both of the coins in the offering. She gave everything she had!

Jesus called to His disciples and told them, "Did you see that woman? What I tell you is true. She put more into the offering than anybody else."

How could that be? the disciples must have wondered. The rich man before her put in a whole sack of money!

Jesus replied, "The amount the rich man gave was tiny compared to the money he has left. But the woman, even though she is poor, put in everything she has."

Dear God,

Thank You for providing for us. Please help us always trust You with everything we have. Amen.

The Lamb of God

(Matthew 26:17-29; Mark 14:12-25;
Luke 22:7-20; John 13:1-20)

Just before it was time for Jesus to die,
He had one last supper with His disciples.
He wanted them to always remember
Him and what He was about to do for
the whole world.

Ever since God helped Moses and the
Israelites escape from slavery in Egypt, the
Jewish people have celebrated the Passover—
when the Israelites put the blood of a lamb
over the doors of their houses in Egypt so that
they would be safe from the last plague.

Jesus loved His disciples, but He knew the time
had come for Him to leave them and this world
and return to His Father in heaven.

Soon after they arrived in Jerusalem, the
disciples asked Jesus where He wanted to
eat the Passover meal. "A man carrying a jar
of water will show you the house," Jesus told
them.

In an upper room of the house, Jesus washed His disciples' feet. He was showing them that the reason He came to earth was to be a servant and to give His life for others.

After they had gathered around a table, Jesus told His friends that one of them would turn Him over to be killed. The disciples were very sad to hear this and wondered who it could be.

It was Judas who would betray Jesus. Jesus told him, "Do quickly what you are going to do." So Judas left.

Jesus held up a loaf of bread. He thanked God for it and said, "This is My body that is broken for you. Take and eat. Every time you do, remember Me."

Jesus then held up a cup of wine. He thanked God for it and said, "This is My blood that will be poured out to forgive the sins of many. Take and drink. Every time you do, remember Me."

Jesus was the new Passover lamb. He was the Lamb of God who would take away the sins of the world.

Dear God,

Thank You for sending Jesus to take away our sins. Please help us always remember Him and what He has done for us. Amen.

A Lonely Night in the Garden

(Matthew 26:30, 36-56; Mark 14:26, 32-52;
Luke 22:39-53; John 18:1-12)

Did you know that Jesus was willing to do what God wanted, even when He knew how difficult it would be?

After the Last Supper, Jesus and all the disciples, except Judas, sang a hymn and went out to the Mount of Olives, a hillside near Jerusalem covered with olive trees. There, Jesus told His disciples that by the time the night was over, they would all leave Him and He would be alone.

Then they walked down the hillside to the Garden of Gethsemane. Knowing that He would die soon, Jesus was very sad. He took His friends Peter, James, and John with Him. He asked if they would stay with Him and keep watch while He prayed.

Jesus prayed, "Father, everything is possible for You. I don't want to suffer, but do what You want, not what I want."

Then an angel appeared to help Him.

When Jesus came back to Peter, James, and John, He found them sleeping.

He woke them up and asked them to pray for Him and keep watch while He spent more time with His Father.

Two more times Jesus returned to find them sleeping.

Peter, James, and John felt ashamed that they could not stay awake for Jesus. Jesus told them, "Get up. Judas is coming to turn Me in."

Judas appeared, followed by a crowd carrying swords and clubs. Before, Judas had told the guards, "The one I kiss is the one you will arrest." He kissed Jesus on the cheek, and the guards grabbed Jesus.

Immediately Peter pulled out a
sword and cut off the ear of one
of the men. Jesus told Peter to
put his sword away.

"If I asked for help to escape, My Father would send it, but this is what must happen."

As Jesus healed the man, all the disciples ran away and left Him alone, just as Jesus had said they would do.

Dear God,

Like Jesus prayed, with You, all things are possible. Please help us do not what we want but what You want. Amen.

Jesus Dies

(Matthew 27; Mark 15; Luke 22:66-71; John 18:28-19:42)

Did you know the reason Jesus came to earth was to give His life for us?

Jesus was brought from the Garden of Gethsemane to Caiaphas, the high priest, and other religious leaders.

Caiaphas demanded that Jesus tell them if He was the Messiah, the Son of God.

When Jesus said that He was, Caiaphas and the other leaders became very angry. They did not believe Him and told Jesus that He must die.

However, the religious leaders did not have the authority to put Jesus to death, so they tied Him up and brought Him to the Roman governor, Pilate.

Pilate didn't think Jesus had done anything wrong, but he did not want to upset the large crowd of people who were angry that Jesus had claimed to be the Messiah.

They shouted, "Crucify Him!" So Pilate ordered that Jesus be nailed to a cross. This was a Roman punishment reserved for the very worst criminals.

Jesus was treated very badly by the Roman soldiers.

They whipped Him and made fun of Him.

The soldiers dressed Him in a purple robe. They twisted thorns together to make a crown and put it on Jesus's head.

They laughed and shouted, "Hail, King of the Jews!" and beat Him.

Then they took off the purple robe and led Jesus away.

The soldiers made Jesus carry His cross through the streets on the way to Golgotha, which means "the Place of the Skull."

When Jesus arrived at Golgotha, the soldiers attached Him to the cross by driving nails into His hands and feet.

Then they pushed up the cross and waited for Jesus to die.

Jesus hung on the cross for many hours. It was very painful for Him.

He could have called an army of angels to save Him, but He knew this was why He had come—to give His life so that we could live with God forever.

Finally, when the land was covered in darkness, Jesus cried out, "My God, My God, why have You left Me?"

And then He died.

A man named Joseph of Arimathea wrapped Jesus's body in clean cloths and placed Him in a tomb cut out of rock.

Joseph then rolled a heavy stone over the entrance of the tomb.

Dear God,

Thank You for loving us so much that You sent Your Son, Jesus, to die for us so that we can live with You in heaven forever. Amen.

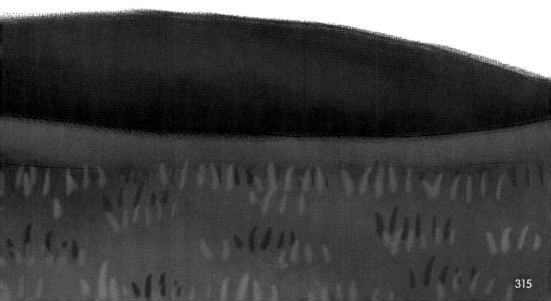

Jesus Is Alive!

(Matthew 28:1-15; Mark 16:1-12; Luke 24; John 20)

Did you know that Jesus defeated the power
of death? Jesus gave His earthly life
to give us eternal life!

After Jesus's death on Friday, Pilate ordered his men to put a seal on Jesus's tomb and placed guards outside of it. Pilate wanted to make sure no one would steal Jesus's body and claim He had been raised from the dead.

Early Sunday morning, as the sun was rising, Mary Magdalene and two other women came to Jesus's tomb.

Suddenly there was a powerful earthquake. An angel appeared from heaven and rolled away the heavy stone. The guards were so afraid of the angel that they were frozen stiff! The women rushed past the guards and entered the tomb.

"Don't be afraid," the angel said. "You are looking for Jesus who was crucified. But He is not here! He is risen!"

The women ran to the disciples and told them what they had seen.

The disciples did not believe them. *How could this be?* they wondered.

Peter got up and ran to the tomb, and the others followed.

When he entered the tomb, Peter saw the clothes that Jesus's body had been wrapped in, but Jesus's body was gone.

What is going on? Peter thought.

Mary stood outside, crying. She turned to see a man standing next to her.

"Why are you crying?" He asked.

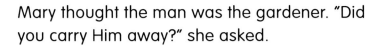

Mary thought the man was the gardener. "Did you carry Him away?" she asked.

But the man was not the gardener. It was Jesus!

He said her name, "Mary." She immediately knew the man was Jesus. Mary was amazed. "Teacher!" she cried out.

Later that night, as most of the disciples gathered in the same room where they had eaten with Jesus, the Lord appeared to them. "Peace be with you!" Jesus said, and then He showed them His hands and side.

The disciples were very happy to see Him!

Dear God,

Thank You for sending us Your Son, Jesus! We praise You because He defeated death! Thank You for forgiving our sins and welcoming us into Your family. Thank You that we are Your children. Amen.

The Good News

(Matthew 28:16-20)

If you heard the best news in the world,
wouldn't you want to tell everyone?

After Jesus rose on Easter morning, He stayed on earth for forty days. During that time, He visited the disciples around Jerusalem and Galilee.

One of those visits was on a mountainside by the Sea of Galilee. Jesus appeared before the eleven disciples, and they worshiped Him.

He had been their friend and teacher for several years, and now most of Jesus's disciples were sure He was the Son of God.

The time had come for Jesus to give them a very important instruction: "Tell the whole world about Me!"

Jesus told the disciples that He had been given all authority in heaven and on earth. He now gave His disciples the responsibility to make more disciples all over the world.

"Baptize them in the name of the Father, and the Son, and the Holy Spirit, and teach them to do everything I have taught you to do," He said. "You can be sure that I will always be with you to the very end."

The disciples had seen Jesus perform many miracles, and they had listened to His teaching about the kingdom of God.

They knew how much He loved everyone and wanted them to turn from the wrong things they had done and be forgiven so that they could be with Him forever in heaven.

This is the good news that Jesus wanted His disciples to share.

Dear God,

Thank You for the good news of Jesus. Please help us tell others about all that You have done so that everyone can know Him! Amen.

Jesus Goes to Heaven

(Luke 24; Acts 1)

The disciples didn't just wait on Jesus—
they went out and got to work!

After Jesus gave the disciples their mission to tell the world about Him, He blessed them. He told them to wait in Jerusalem for the gift, the Helper, that God had promised. Then He lifted His hands and spoke blessings over all of them, His dear friends who had followed Him and served Him throughout His time on earth.

While He was still blessing them, He began to rise into the sky.

The disciples watched in awe as a cloud carried Jesus—their teacher, their leader, their Savior, their friend—away. They stared into the sky until they could not see Him any longer. Jesus had gone back to heaven.

As they stood there, still looking up, two men dressed in brilliant white appeared. "Why are you still standing there staring at the sky?" they asked. "Yes, Jesus has gone to heaven. But He's going to come back in the same way that you saw Him go."

The disciples looked at each other and remembered Jesus's last instructions to them. So together, they set off for Jerusalem to wait for the Helper that Jesus had promised. As they walked and as they waited, they celebrated, praising and worshiping Jesus for the time that they had with Him and for all He had done.

Dear Jesus,

Thank You for the time You spent here on earth, setting a perfect example of how to live. Help us always remember the instructions You gave and the love You shared. Amen.

The Disciples Spread the Word

(Acts 2-3, 9, 12, 16)

The disciples were excited to spread the word of Jesus. They spoke boldly, and many came to believe!

The disciples were all together in Jerusalem when a huge gust of heavenly wind swept through the house. In that moment, the disciples were all filled with the Holy Spirit, the Helper that Jesus had promised to send to them.

They realized the Holy Spirit was helping them speak in different languages.

A crowd soon gathered, amazed and confused because they could each hear the disciples speaking his own language.

Peter stood up and began to speak to them about Jesus, the Son of God who had given His life to save them. And when the disciples finished talking that day, three thousand people were baptized in the name of Jesus.

But that was just the beginning. The disciples continued to tell people about Jesus and do amazing things. Once when Peter and John were going to the temple, a man who couldn't walk was outside begging. Peter said, "I don't have silver or gold, but I'll give you what I do have. In the name of Jesus, stand up and walk!" That man didn't stand up—he jumped up and went into the temple with them, praising God.

One day when the disciples were preaching by the river, they met a woman named Lydia who sold purple cloth. When she heard about Jesus, she and her whole family were baptized!

A man named Saul was really mean to those who believed in Jesus. One day he was going to Damascus to try to put Christians in jail. Suddenly a bright light flashed, and a voice said, "Saul, why are you being so mean to Me?"

Saul looked up and said, "Who are You?"

"I am Jesus, the One you are hurting," the voice said.

Saul stood up, but he couldn't see. So the men with him helped him into the city.

After three days, the Lord spoke to Ananias, another disciple. "Go find a man named Saul and give him back his sight."

When Ananias did, something like scales fell from Saul's eyes, and he could see again. From then on, he became known as Paul. He joined the disciples in preaching the message of Jesus.

Once Peter was in prison for preaching about Jesus. He was chained between two guards. Suddenly an angel appeared to him. "Hurry! Get up!"

The chains fell from Peter's hands, and he followed the angel out of that prison. He went to Mary's house, where several people were praying for Peter to be set free. He knocked on the door and called, "It's Peter! Let me in!"

"Peter's at the door!" a woman named Rhoda told the group.

"No, he's not," they said. "Peter is in prison."

When they finally answered the door, they were amazed to see Peter standing there, free.

Telling people about Jesus wasn't always easy, but those who believed always had God, Jesus, and the Helper with them.

Dear Jesus,

Help us tell others about You, even when it isn't easy. Thank You for always being with us and helping us when we need You most. Amen.

John Sees Heaven

(Revelation 1, 4, 21)

God showed John a new heaven and a new earth—the place God has prepared for us to live with Him forever!

After a lifetime of telling the world about Jesus, John was sent to an island as a punishment for preaching about Jesus. One Sabbath, the Lord's Day, he heard a voice like a trumpet. It told him to write down everything he saw.

When John turned to see who was speaking, he saw seven lampstands with a man standing in the middle. The man's head and hair were bright white. His eyes were like fire. His feet glowed like hot metal, and his voice sounded like rushing water. His face was like the sun. John fell at His feet.

The man said, "Don't be afraid. I am the beginning and the end, One who was dead and is now alive forever."

He took John to a place in heaven where there was a throne surrounded by a rainbow. On the throne was a man who looked like jewels, like jasper and ruby. Around that throne were twenty-four other thrones with men wearing white robes and gold crowns.

"Holy, holy, holy is the Lord, God Almighty, the One who was, who is, and is to come," they worshiped. "You are worthy, Lord, for You created everything."

Then John was taken to see a new heaven and earth. From a mountain, John saw the city of Jerusalem shining as clear as crystal. It was surrounded by a tall wall with twelve gates and twelve angels.

And the One who sat on the throne said, "Here, God will live with His people, and they will be His. He will wipe every tear from their eyes. There will be no crying, no pain, and no death. See, I am making everything new."

The city didn't need a sun or a moon. It was lit completely by the glory of God. And only the people who were written in the book of life would be there in the new heaven and earth that God created.

Dear Jesus,

Thank You for creating a new heaven and earth for us. Thank You for caring enough to make all things new. Please help us follow You so we can have our name written in the book of life and live with You forever. Amen.

Dear Child,

We hope that you have learned so much about God and how very much He loves you.

The most important way God showed His love for us was when He sent His only Son to pay the price for our sins. When we realize that we've done wrong, we need to turn away from those sins and turn toward Jesus and His love instead. If you believe this is true and haven't already chosen to accept that gift of forgiveness, you can do it now by reading scriptures like Romans 9:9–10 and Acts 16:30–34 with your parents and by praying this simple prayer:

> Dear Jesus,
>
> I believe that You are the Son of God and that You died to save me from my sins. Without Your sacrifice, my sins, all the wrong things I've done, would cost me my life in heaven with You. But You have already paid that price. I want to accept Your gift now. Please forgive me of my sins and show me how to live for You. Amen.

If you've said that prayer (or one like it), you have accepted the gift of salvation. You have been saved by Jesus. You can live your life for Him on earth and spend eternity with Him in heaven. That big gift may come with a lot more questions, and that's completely normal. Keep reading your Bible, spend time in God's house, and ask your parents, teachers, and leaders any questions you may have.

Most of all, seek God and trust God, knowing that He will reveal Himself to you, now and forever.

We are praying for you!

Mike & Amy